ROGER CLEMENS ★ DARRYL STRAWBERRY

RICHARD J. BRENNER

LYNX BOOKS

New York

ROGER CLEMENS * DARRYL STRAWBERRY

ISBN: 1-55802-333-X

First Printing/April 1989

Cover Photos:
Roger Clemens front and back cover and Darryl
Strawberry back cover: Mitchell B. Reibel,
SportsChrome East/West.

Darryl Strawberry front cover: Ron Wyatt,
SportsChrome East/West

This book is published by Lynx Books, a division of Lynx
Communications, Inc., 41 Madison Avenue, New York,
New York, 10010. The name "Lynx" and the logo consisting
of a stylized head of a lynx are trademarks of Lynx
Communications, Inc.

Printed in the United States of America

0 9 8 7 6 5 4 3 2 1

DEDICATION

With great love for Halle and Jason and Anita. Thank you for your help and encouragement.

To the special feeling of warm days in center field and the joy of a line drive into the gap. And to the boys of the Avenue P Park in Brooklyn who shared those moments with me. With love to my mother, who always understood the missed meals, thank you. And with love to Aunt Es and Uncle Sam, thanks for all that you have always given.

And finally, to Milton and Helen Kern, who bought me my first baseball glove, a PMM. And to Carole Kulikowsky, my favorite librarian.

The author wishes to acknowledge the following:

Darryl! by Darryl Strawberry with Dan Castellano
Esquire Magazine
Inside Sports
The Los Angeles Times
Newsday
The New York Times
People Weekly
Rocket Man: The Roger Clemens Story by Roger
    Clemens with Peter Gammons
Sports Illustrated
The World Series: The Great Contests by Richard J.
    Brenner

ROGER CLEMENS ★ DARRYL STRAWBERRY

ROGER CLEMENS

1

Something Special

"I always loved hard throwers and strikeouts. After Nolan Ryan signed with the Astros, I'd go to the Dome to watch him pitch. I'd sit down by the bullpen when he'd warm up. There was never anyone there, and I loved the sound the fastball made in the glove."

William Roger Clemens was born August 4, 1962, in Dayton, Ohio. He was the fifth child of Bess and Bill Clemens. Shortly after he was born, though, Bess took Roger and the other children—Rick, Randy, Brenda, and Janet—and left Bill Clemens. Two years later Bess married a man named Woody Booher and the family moved to the small town of Vandalia, Ohio.

Roger has good memories of growing up in a loving family, which grew to six children when his sister Bonnie was born. They lived in a big house with a large yard and a pool. And best of all they had a barn, and everyone had their own horse. They even had an old buggy, and when it snowed, the family would pile in and go for rides around the countryside. And Woody always seemed to have time to take the kids for rides on his motorcycle. "He gave us everything we could ask for," remembers Roger.

But when Roger was nine, Woody died. "His death was tough for all of us," reports Roger, "because he was such a great man and worked very hard to make us all happy." It was about that same time that Roger realized that he had a biological father. But the information didn't seem to interest him. Roger never saw Bill Clemens, who died in 1981, and the only time that he heard his voice was over a telephone wire once when Roger was ten. "I consider Woody to be my father."

After Woody died, Roger's older brother Randy looked out for him. When Randy, who was a gifted athlete himself, saw that Roger was talented in baseball, he made sure that Roger had enough competition by getting him into leagues with older boys. Roger's mom was also an early believer. "I remember watching him pitch in Little League when he was nine. He struck out the side on nine pitches, and the catcher's glove made a popping noise. That's when I thought we had something special in the family."

By the time Roger was ready to start tenth grade, the family resettled in Sugartown, right outside of Houston, Texas. Roger, the new kid from a small town in Ohio, was at first uneasy about attending Dolles High School, which was the largest high school in Texas. As Roger says, "I was intimidated."

But once the baseball season started, Roger began to feel comfortable. He was initially assigned to the junior varsity, but before long he was called up to the varsity and compiled a 12–1 record. "I thought I was a hotshot."

But his brother Randy thought that Roger needed stronger competition. Randy took Roger to see a regional play-off game between two schools that he thought had good baseball programs. "After the game," he told Roger, "I want you to tell me which school you want to go to." Spring Woods High School lost the game, 4–2, but Roger picked them anyway. And by the time Roger was ready to start his junior year, the family had moved into the Spring Woods school district.

During that summer Roger, as usual, was playing in as many baseball leagues as he could. He was on four different teams and playing as many as ten games a week.

4

Roger would usually pitch four times a week, which is probably more often than he should have, and the rest of the time he would play shortstop or first base.

As soon as school started, though, Roger traded in his baseball cap for a football helmet and shoulder pads. Roger, who was already 6′ 1″ and over 200 pounds, put his bulk and determination to use as a defensive end.

But as soon as the first signs of spring returned, Roger was out throwing a baseball. Even back then Roger had excellent control, but he didn't have much of a fastball. Roger could throw his hummer at about only 80 miles per hour, and since there were two talented seniors who could hum theirs at around 90 MPH, Roger had to settle for the number-three spot in the pitching rotation. But Roger worked hard and made the most of his opportunities and talent; and in one game he used his excellent control to set a school strikeout record by fanning eighteen.

In his senior season Roger had a 13–5 record, but college recruiters and professional scouts weren't impressed because there wasn't much fuel in Roger's heater. He didn't receive a full scholarship offer from any university, and none of the major-league teams drafted him. A scout from the Minnesota Twins did offer to sign him to a pro contract but warned Roger, "If you don't sign now, you'll never get the chance to play again." Roger's mom quickly showed that scout the door.

Roger ran down to the Spring Woods pitcher's mound and lay down, wondering about his future. Then he closed himself in his room for two days and wondered some more.

2

Almost a Met

Roger finally stopped wondering and accepted a scholarship offer from coach Wayne Graham of San Jacinto Junior College. Coach Graham liked Roger's "near-genius control" and felt that Roger would throw bullets if he just worked on the follow-through of his pitching motion.

When Roger arrived at San Jacinto JC, coach Graham kept reminding him to "finish strong, finish strong." By the time spring training began, Roger had grown to 6' 4", and during the season he perfected his follow-through. And then one day it happened. Roger broke 90 MPH for the first time. He kept getting stronger throughout the season and finished with a 9–2 record and 82 strikeouts in 85 2/3 innings.

Randy thought that Roger was now ready for stiffer competition, and should move up to the university level. And Roger, now that he had the heater, had become a hot prospect. The University of Texas baseball coach, Cliff Gustafson, who a year earlier had thought that Roger wasn't any better than "very mediocre," offered him a full scholarship. Roger accepted, but only after coach Gus agreed that Roger could pitch the nationally televised opening game against Miami and the home opener against Texas A&M.

Roger, though, almost didn't make it to Austin to pitch for the Longhorns, because the New York Mets picked Roger in the twelfth round of the 1981 major-league draft. When the Mets came to Houston to play the Astros, they invited Roger to come to the Astrodome and work out in front of their manager, Joe Torre, and pitching coach, Bob

Gibson. Roger was thrilled. He was going to be throwing in the Astrodome, where he had gone so often to hear Nolan Ryan pop the fastball.

Roger was given a Mets uniform and did his throwing. But Torre and Gibson weren't too impressed with what they saw. The Mets did make an offer, but it was low and Roger rejected it. Jim Terrell, the local Mets scout, wasn't ready to give up, though. He had seen Roger pitch a number of times, and he was convinced that Roger was a major-league prospect. He kept calling the Mets' office in New York until they raised their offer. But it still wasn't the number that Roger wanted. Then Terrell convinced their scouting director, Joe McIlvaine, to fly to Houston and check Roger out himself under game conditions. But on the weekend that McIlvaine flew to Houston, it rained both days. And when he returned the following weekend, it rained some more. McIlvaine didn't have the time to return a third time for a twelfth-round draft choice. The Mets' final offer was only $5,000 less than what Roger was asking, but neither side would budge. And that $5,000 is how close the Mets came to having Roger on the same pitching staff as Dwight Gooden, David Cone, and Ron Darling!

So instead of heading off for some minor-league town, Roger was on his way to Austin. The University of Texas has one of the very best college baseball programs in the country. They recruit top-flight talent, and their appearance in Omaha, where the College World Series is played, is an almost annual event. On the team with Roger that year were Spike Owen, Calvin Schiraldi, and thirteen other players who would get drafted by major-league teams in the two years that Roger pitched there.

Roger had a super season, going 15–2, and the Longhorns made their semi-automatic appearance in Omaha for the College World Series. Roger pitched well in the final game, but Texas fell to the University of Miami, 2–1.

The following year Roger and Calvin and some of the other Longhorns found themselves on the cover of national sports magazines that told them what terrific players they were and that Texas was the number-one college team in the country.

But when the season started, the team fizzled. Roger got cuffed around in his first few outings and Calvin Schiraldi also got stomped on. Finally coach Gus suggested that the players reread the magazine stories that had told them how good they were and start playing ball. The team got the message and got itself on track. With Roger and Calvin leading the way, the Longhorns began to roll, and the victories began to mount. Roger finished up with a 13–5 record and a 3.04 earned run average. And in allowing only 22 walks while striking out 151 batters, Roger demonstrated a rare combination: a power pitcher with exceptional control. Calvin did his part by finishing up at 14–2 with a 1.74 ERA and was selected as the Baseball America College Pitcher of the Year.

The Longhorns then went on to win their NCAA regional tournament as Roger pitched them past Mississippi State. State was led by Will Clark, now the slugging first baseman of the San Francisco Giants who in 1988 led the National League in RBIs, and Rafael Palmeiro, the sweet-stroking outfielder.

The victory earned the Longhorns a trip up to Omaha to compete in the College World Series. It was a doubly exciting and nerve-racking time for the players who hoped to make baseball their career, because it was also the week that major-league baseball staged its annual draft of high-school and college players.

Roger thought that he might be selected by the Texas Rangers, who had the third pick, or the Astros, who owned the eighth selection. But eighteen teams passed him by before the Red Sox tapped him as the nineteenth selection in the draft. Roger was surprised and a little disappointed. He thought that he would be selected earlier and be able to play in Texas. "As far as I was concerned, Boston was a foreign country." Ed Kenney, Boston's director of player development, was also surprised, but he was delighted. "It baffles me as to why there wouldn't be more interest in a guy who throws as hard as he does and still throws strikes."

But Roger tucked his disappointment away that night and pitched Texas past Oklahoma State, 9–1. And later in the week, after Schiraldi had pitched the Longhorns to within one victory of the championship, Roger was given the ball to wrap it up against the University of Alabama. Roger was stung early when Dave Magadan, a great college hitter and currently an infielder for the New York Mets, lined a two-run double to give Alabama a 2–0 lead. But Texas battled back, Roger hung tough, and the Longhorns won the game 4–3 and the 1983 College World Series.

After the game Roger signed with the Red Sox for $121,000, and the journey toward Boston was begun.

3

Fast Track to Fenway

Roger was assigned to the Red Sox farm team in Winter
Haven, Florida. For some ballplayers, especially high
schoolers, starting out in professional baseball is a tremendous thrill, but for Roger it was almost a letdown. He'd had
two years at the University of Texas with its first-class
stadium and carpeted locker room and had just finished up
in Omaha, playing for a championship in front of a packed
stadium every day. In Winter Haven the field didn't
measure up to what Roger was used to playing on, the
locker room was spartan, and there were never more than a
hundred people in the stands. Roger was also disappointed
by the lack of rigorous training techniques and the fact that
the hitters he was facing in A ball weren't any better than
the batters he had faced in college. The biggest challenge
was surviving the Texas-sized, man-eating swarms of bugs
that showed up on the field every night.

One day they even faced an aerial bombardment, when a
sea gull dropped a fish it was carrying toward the light
tower in center field, where the bird nested. Either the fish
was too heavy for the bird or the gull just wanted to start a
food fight with first baseman Jeff Ledbetter, who just
missed getting beaned.

Roger made certain that he wouldn't have to spend too
much time in Winter Haven by simply overpowering
opposing batters. He started four games, completed the last
three, compiled a 3–1 record, allowed only four runs in 29
innings, struck out 36, and didn't walk a single batter.
After the fourth game, in which Roger threw goose eggs

and fanned 15, he got a phone call from Ed Kenney. "Pack your bags," Kenney told Roger, "you've just been promoted to the Red Sox' Double A team in New Britain, Connecticut."

Roger responded to the challenge and helped pitch New Britain into the Eastern League play-offs. He rang up a 4–1 record with an excellent 1.38 ERA while striking out 59 batters and walking only 12 in 52 innings.

In the opening round of the play-offs, Roger pitched brilliantly against the favored Reading nine. He gave up only three hits and one run and notched fifteen Ks. In the finals against the Lynn Pirates, Roger was asked to close out the series, and he responded by tossing a three-hit shutout and striking out ten.

It had been quite a summer for the young fireballer. He had won 17 games for the Longhorns and then gone 9–2 while compiling a nifty 1.19 ERA with 108 Ks in his first season of professional ball. He had pitched the college championship game in Omaha, and less than three months later he had hurled the clincher for New Britain.

But before he got to go back home and get some rest and enjoy what he had accomplished, he got another call from Ed Kenney. The American League season was still in progress, and the Red Sox thought it would be a good idea if he came to Boston to get acquainted with the team, the city, and fabled Fenway Park.

Fenway Park, the oldest baseball park in the American League, was built in 1912. Unlike today's modern stadiums, which all look pretty much alike, Fenway was built at a time when ballparks were designed with unique characteristics. What stands out most about Fenway, especially for nervous young pitchers, is the left-field wall. It is only 315 feet from home plate, which allows a lot of doubles to be hit off it and home runs to be hit over it. A lot of the home runs that get hit in Fenway would only be fly balls in any other park. The left-field wall is painted green and is known as "The Green Monster" or simply "The Wall."

Roger's mom told him not to be concerned with The Wall. "They can't hit what they can't see," she reasoned encouragingly.

When Roger walked into the clubhouse, he was delighted to see that there was a locker waiting for him that had a Boston jersey hanging in it with his number 21 on the back. It was no secret where the Red Sox expected Roger to be hurling the next season.

4

Bright Promise, False Start

Roger, to no one's great surprise, was invited to spring training with the Red Sox in 1984. When Roger reported to camp he was already in pretty good shape. He's always been a big believer in physical fitness and follows a year-long program that includes running, weight lifting, sit-ups, and throwing. Roger was amazed that the training program that the Red Sox followed wasn't very vigorous. "By the third week I was in worse shape than when I reported." So Roger quickly returned to following his own, more demanding regimen.

Roger thought that he had thrown well in the exhibition games and had a good chance to make it up to Boston. But Ralph Houk, who was managing the Red Sox, told Roger that he was being sent to their Class AAA team in Pawtucket, Rhode Island. Roger, of course, was disappointed. He suspected, though, that the decision might have had more to do with finances than talent. If Roger had started the season in Boston, he would be eligible, because of the rules concerning salary arbitration, to make more money sooner than if he had started off in the majors.

On May 11, after only six starts, the call came to come to Boston. Roger's record was only 2–3, but he had a sparkling 1.93 ERA and was striking out batters at a rate of more than one an inning.

Roger got his first major-league start four days later, in Cleveland. His mom and his sister Bonnie flew up from Houston, and his brother Randy and his wife drove up from where they were living in Ohio. The big day had finally arrived, but Roger couldn't really appreciate it. "I

13

have never been more nervous than that first start in Cleveland." And it showed. Roger gave up a run in the first inning and four more before Houk gave him the hook after only 5 2/3 innings. Besides the five runs, Roger surrendered three walks and allowed six stolen bases to a team that, at the time, was battling Boston for last place. The only good part for Roger was that Boston tied the score before they finally lost so at least he didn't get saddled with the loss. It was not a storybook start.

But Roger pitched better in his next outing. He went seven innings against the Twins, struck out seven, and got the credit for his first major-league victory, 5–4, when Bob Stanley pitched two perfect innings in relief.

Roger was in and out in his next few starts. He pitched fairly well against the Royals but wound up with a no-decision when the bullpen couldn't hold a 5–3 lead. Then he came back and picked up a 6–3 win against the Brewers despite a pair of dingers by Robin Yount. But Milwaukee evened the score in a big way in Roger's next game, touching him for 13 hits and six runs in 5 2/3 innings and pinning his first loss on him. Roger was not any better in his next start, against the Yankees. The Bronx Bombers pounded him for six early runs and knocked him out of the game, but Roger was lucky and avoided the loss when Boston bounced back for the win, 9–8.

Roger wasn't used to getting roughed up, and the experience dented his confidence and caused him to lose his concentration on the mound. Instead of just focusing in on what he should do with the baseball, he was worrying about what the hitters could do with their bats. "I wasn't seeing any holes; I was pitching defensively."

Lee Stange, who was the Red Sox pitching coach, sat Roger down and told him to just relax and concentrate on throwing. "With your stuff and control, if you just let it go, you'll win. It's as simple as that. Even if you get hammered in your next start, you're not going anywhere. You'll still get your next start. You're here. Period."

In addition to the confidence-building pep talk, Stange also made two useful suggestions. One, that Roger should throw fewer strikes and try to get hitters to swing at balls out of the strike zone. The theory is simple. The closer a pitch is to the strike zone, the closer it is to most batters' hitting zones. The best pitchers are almost always those pitchers who can move the ball in and out and up and down and just hit the corners of the plate. What Stange was suggesting was that Roger had such good movement on his pitches and threw with such velocity that he could pitch off the plate, far away from the batters' hitting zones, and still get them to swing because his velocity forced hitters into having to commit to swing in a fraction of a second. Stange also suggested that Roger should start throwing a four-seam curveball, which helped Roger throw a better breaking ball.

The talk and the suggestions seemed to produce immediate results, because in his next outing Roger held the Blue Jays to one hit while striking out seven before rain washed the game away. Five days later, though, there were no showers to save the Jays, and Roger blew them away 9–1.

But then Roger hit the roughest patch of road he had ever known. He started four games, lost three, and had a no-decision. His record for the year was down to 3–4, his ERA had ballooned up to 5.94, and the league's batting average against Roger was .326.

The only good thing that happened during the stretch was that Roger finally got to pitch to the one person he had dreamed of pitching against: Reggie Jackson. Roger fanned Reggie twice, but his third time up Roger tried challenging him again, and Reggie rocketed one of Roger's fastballs into the bleachers.

Reporters began writing stories suggesting that the Red

Sox had rushed Roger to the big leagues before he was ready and that he could use some more time at Pawtucket. Ralph Houk, the Boston manager, told Roger to forget the stories. "You're a good major-league pitcher. You ain't going anywhere."

Houk took Roger out of the rotation for one turn to relieve the pressure, and just had him work on his mechanics by throwing on the sideline. "What I worked out on the sideline was more mental than physical. I simply got my thinking straight and regained my concentration." Then Houk put Roger in for two innings of relief work as a little confidence booster. The following week he returned Roger to the starting rotation and watched him rack up six straight wins.

He began the streak by blanking the White Sox for his first major-league shutout. It was his first win in 34 days. He beat the White Sox again, then the Tigers, and then the Rangers in front of a rooting section of family and friends in Dallas. Next he knocked off Kansas City 11–1, fanning 15 Royals without giving up a base on balls. He became only the fourth pitcher ever to strike out 15 or more batters without issuing a walk. Roger won his sixth straight against Cleveland, a three-hit, ten-K beauty. The win improved his record to 9–4 and helped him earn the selection as the American League pitcher of the month for August.

Roger was on his way to another win against Cleveland on the last day of August when he suddenly felt a sharp pain in his right forearm and had to leave the game. It was scary at the time, but it turned out to be minor. Roger was all set to take the mound ten days later, but the Boston management decided that since it was late in the season and the Red Sox didn't have a chance at first place anyway, it might be best if Roger didn't pitch any more that year.

But Roger had finished up his rookie season in style by

winning six straight, and the Red Sox had finished strongly. Everyone was optimistic and looking forward to 1985.

In the off-season Roger took enough time off from his usual training regime to get married and honeymoon in Hawaii. The Red Sox also made some changes during the winter, so when Roger reported to spring training, he met a new manager, John McNamara, and a new pitching coach, Bill Fischer.

Fischer was responsible for teaching Roger how to throw a new pitch by showing him another way to grip his fastball. The new pitch, the cross-seam fastball, rose up suddenly as it crossed the plate. The new pitch gave batters something else to be concerned with, since Roger's other fastball, the one he threw with the seams, either sinks or runs away or tails in to batters. Being able to go up and down as well as in and out had a great effect on Roger's pitching and a devastating impact on hitters. "It seemed to make the strike zone larger," noted Roger.

Roger started off the season slowly, though, and didn't really kick it into gear until mid-May, when he threw a shutout at Cleveland. The win raised Roger's record to 3–4, but it was during that game that he first began to feel pain in his right shoulder. Roger tried to pitch through the pain in his next turn, against the Twins. "I felt that I was forcing myself, that I wasn't right." But instead of bowing out, Roger tried to turn it on. The Twins were putting the radar readings up on the Metrodome scoreboard, and when Roger saw it register 97 MPH, he tried to reach back and throw even harder, kick it up to 98, 99, maybe even break 100. Not surprisingly, after the game the pain was more intense, and now, finally, Roger was worried. But instead of sitting down, Roger took a few more turns on the mound. Finally, on July 7, as he was warming up to pitch a game against the Angels in Anaheim, Fischer and McNamara told him to forget it. "Pack your bags and fly back to Boston for treatment," they told him.

Roger went back to the clubhouse, tearful and angry, thinking, "Why me?" He thought that if he couldn't throw the fastball anymore, then maybe he could get by with his excellent control and a trick pitch, maybe a knuckleball; or maybe he could go back to Winter Haven and try to make it as a first baseman. Roger felt his life unraveling just at the point when he thought it should all be coming together. "I couldn't stand being one of those could-have-beens. I really was hurting."

Roger was placed on the disabled list for a month, but the team doctor wasn't able to discover the cause of the pain. Roger kept working out and throwing on the sideline, but he wasn't able to maintain the velocity on his fastball.

Roger came off the DL in early August and tried pitching against the Royals. But by the fourth inning he felt the shoulder going again. Roger, feeling frustrated and fearful, foolishly took his next regular turn against the Yankees. He toughed it out for five innings, but even the umpire noticed that something was wrong with his motion. McNamara finally took the ball out of his hand and put an end to Roger's scary second season.

But fortunately for Roger, a specialist discovered that Roger's problem was only a small piece of loose cartilage in his shoulder. The surgery to remove the cartilage was quick and easy, but the doctor told Roger that the recovery would depend upon how hard Roger was willing to work to rehabilitate the shoulder. The doctor also told Roger that he probably would never have received the injury if he had known about and done the proper shoulder exercises when he was younger.

5

The Rocket Roars

Roger was back home and on the rehab program the very next day, and he was, as always, very diligent about his exercising and conditioning program. But when he arrived at spring training he began working even harder. As catcher Rich Gedman pointed out, "He had good work habits before the injury, but he was like a man possessed after it. It seemed like he felt, 'Here's my second chance, and I'm not going to let it slip away.'"

But Roger was afraid to cut loose with the fastball, afraid he would feel the pain in the shoulder again. Bill Fischer, who knew that the shoulder was sound, told Roger, "You're a fastball pitcher. Go out there and air it out."

In his last exhibition outing, Roger decided to do it. "I made up my mind that day that I was going to let it fly and air it out and not hold anything back. If I got two strikes on batters, I was going to try to throw it by them."

Roger, throwing as fast as 95 MPH, threw it by a lot of Astros that day. He knew that he was back. The Rocket was fueled. And he was also confident that the Red Sox were going to surprise all the experts who had predicted a fifth-place finish for them.

Roger got off to a rousing start in his first outing of the 1986 season. He went 8 2/3 innings against the White Sox and picked up his first win. In his next outing he pitched a complete game and, with backing from Don Baylor's grand slam, beat the Royals 6–2. Roger still didn't feel absolutely sharp, but he felt like it was coming together again. Roger's next start was against the Tigers, and after picking up his third straight win and racking up ten Ks, Roger knew that he was all the way back.

When Roger woke up on April 29, he had a king-size headache and felt edgy all day. He went to Fenway and went through his usual pregame rituals. And then he went to the bullpen to warm up for his start against the Seattle Mariners. The midweek game against the meek Mariners didn't provoke much excitement in Boston, and only 13,414 showed up to watch it. It was just another Tuesday night in Beantown. But before the night was over, Rocket would put on a performance that would light up the scoreboard and rewrite the record book.

Roger, his fastball popping, began the game by striking out the side, starting with his former Longhorn teammate Spike Owen. After he had gone around the Seattle order for the first time, he had six strikeouts and was working on a perfect game.

Spike Owen put an end to the perfect game, though, when he singled off a wicked breaking ball. "That was one of my best curveballs of the year." But Roger, relying mostly on his fastball, struck out the side, with a little assist from first baseman Don Baylor, who dropped a foul ball. Roger came right back and fanned the side in the fifth, too, to give him six consecutive Ks and a total of 12. He started the sixth by striking out Dave Henderson with a wicked sinker and then got Steve Yeager with a breaking pitch to run his total to fourteen. Roger's fastball was really running, but he wanted to show the curve enough to keep the hitters off balance. The pitch surprised Yeager so much that he never moved his bat. The pesky Owen broke the streak of strikeouts at eight, a new American League record, when he lined out.

Roger was in another zone at this point. He had near-total concentration. The only sight he saw was Rich Gedman behind the plate flashing the signs and setting his catcher's mitt as a target. It was total tunnel vision. Roger didn't see the crowd or hear their cheering. He didn't even notice who was up at bat.

He started the seventh inning by fanning Phil Bradley and Ken Phelps to run his total to sixteen. But Gorman Thomas broke the spell, broke up the shutout, and gave Seattle a 1–0 lead with one swish of his bat. Roger quickly restored order, though, by getting the next hitter to ground out to first.

Roger received two big boosts in the bottom of the seventh inning. First, the boy who usually hung the K cards when Roger pitched showed up and strung up sixteen squares. Then Dwight Evans took care of the fact that Roger was at the short end of a 1–0 game by poling a two-out, three-run homer. Roger was so excited that when Evans reached the dugout, Roger jumped on him and knocked Dwight to the ground.

Roger, really pumped up now, went out in the eighth inning and struck out two more, including Dave Henderson for the third time, to run his total to eighteen.

When Roger went out to pitch the ninth inning, he had a chance to make baseball history. Only three major-league pitchers—Steve Carlton in 1969, Tom Seaver in 1970, and Nolan Ryan in 1974—had ever struck out 19 batters in a nine-inning game. And that trio of hurlers will be in Cooperstown as soon as they become eligible for the Hall of Fame. That's where Roger was—at the brink of greatness.

As Roger was leaving the dugout, Al Nipper, his friend and teammate, said, "Roger, do you know what you're *doing*? Two more for the record!" A lot of the Boston players were worried that Nipper had added to the tension of the moment, but Nipper just laughed. "Not him, he loves it."

As Roger strode to the mound, the Fenway faithful rose to give him a standing ovation. Spike Owen, who had been a problem for Roger, stepped into the batter's box. Roger didn't need a sign from Gedman; he was throwing only heat. He got ahead on the count and then smoked a cross-seamed fastball that jumped over Owen's bat for strike three.

As the Fenway fans roared their approval, a message lit up the scoreboard: ROGER CLEMENS HAS TIED THE MAJOR-LEAGUE RECORD FOR STRIKEOUTS IN A NINE-INNING GAME WITH 19.

Phil Bradley, whom Roger had already fanned three times, was up next. Roger got two strikes on Bradley as the small crowd made a big noise. Roger went into his windup and sent smoke toward Gedman's glove. Bradley tensed but didn't swing. Plate umpire Vic Voltaggio punched up his right hand and screamed, "Strike three!" Roger had set a new strikeout record. Fenway Park seemed to rock as the crowd raised the volume up to max. Gedman tossed the ball down to third baseman Wade Boggs the way that catchers do after every strikeout. When the ball worked its way back to Wade, he walked over to the mound, dropped it into Roger's glove, and said, "Awesome."

What made this awesome accomplishment even more remarkable was the fact that Roger didn't walk a single batter. Twenty Ks and not one base on balls.

In all the 111 seasons and in all the 147,000 major-league baseball games that had ever been played, that feat had never before been accomplished. As Wade Boggs said, "That's all the perspective I need."

As important as the game was personally for Roger, it also had a great impact on the entire team. As Bruce Hurst, their talented southpaw, observed, "The night that he struck out twenty, everyone was thinking, 'Hey, we've got a weapon that no one else has,' and that night everyone in a Red Sox uniform was convinced that we were going to win the pennant."

Roger kept the heat on in his next start against the A's with a three-hit, ten-K, 4–1 win. It started the Red Sox off on a 12–2 surge that they rode right into first place.

Roger's next start resulted in a no-decision when the bullpen couldn't hold a 5–2 lead in the ninth inning. Roger got lucky in his next outing though. He gave up five walks and five runs, including a monstrous home run by Reggie Jackson. ("Hey," quipped Roger, "it was worth watching.") But his teammates bailed him out as Boggs blasted a two-run homer, Gedman smacked a three-run homer, and Joe Sambito saved the 8–5 win.

Roger upped his record to 7–0 in his next start, a gift from the Boston batters, who mauled Minnesota 17–7. The next stop was in Dallas, and Roger nearly spun another masterpiece in front of a crowd that included lots of friends and relatives. He came within four outs of a no-hitter before light-hitting Oddibe McDowell broke it up with a line-drive single. Then Darrel Porter poled a home run in the bottom of the ninth inning to ruin Roger's shutout, but Roger came away with the win, 7–1.

Roger went to 9–0 with a 6–3 win over the Twins and then to 10–0 when he whitewashed the Brewers, 3–0. Roger picked up number 11 on a cold and rainy night in Toronto and number 12 in an important matchup against the Yankees. Boston went into the Stadium with its lead cut to three and a half games, but Roger quieted the Yanks' bats; the Red Sox romped 10–1 and went on to sweep the three-game series. Roger ran his consecutive-game winning streak to 14 with two victories in six days over the Orioles. Rocket was now only one win away from the American League record for consecutive victories at the start of a season.

Roger pitched brilliantly against the Blue Jays and went into the eighth inning having allowed only one hit (a George Bell home run) and with a 2–1 lead. But then he made two

23

quick mistakes. He walked the leadoff hitter in the inning and he gave up a hit on an 0–2 pitch to the light-hitting Damaso Garcia. Roger picked up an out on an attempted sacrifice, but then Rance Mulliniks sliced a double down the left-field line that tied the game at 2–2 and left runners at second and third. Roger rubbed up the ball, thinking about the batter who was due up. But McNamara decided to go to his bullpen and brought in Bob Stanley.

Roger was angry. He still had his good stuff, he was the hottest pitcher in baseball, and he was going for the record. He thought, and most people would agree, that he had earned the right to win or lose.

With the score tied and two runners on, Roger couldn't win the game anymore; he could only lose it. And he did, when Toronto cashed in the runs against Stanley and won 4–2. The streak was over; mission control had pulled the plug on the Rocket.

The disappointing loss caused Roger to sag, and he came up empty in his next start. But José Canseco and Dave Henderson had plenty of fuel in their bats, and their home runs led the A's to a 6–4 win. Roger was furious with himself. "I get only thirty-four opportunities to pitch, and I'd just thrown one away. I'd let down my teammates and myself." But instead of dwelling on negative feelings, Roger worked them out by running and doing sit-ups; and then in his next start he went out and pitched a complete-game victory.

Red-hot Roger took his 15–2 record back home to Houston as the starting pitcher for the American League's All-Star team. Rocket was all pumped up about his first appearance in the midsummer classic and the chance to perform in front of the hometown folks.

Roger didn't approach the game as if it were an exhibition, as some players had in other All-Star Games. He was determined to help reverse the trend that had seen the American League lose the last two, 13 out of 14, and 21 out of the last 23 games to the National League. He was tired of people treating the AL as if it were Rodney Dangerfield.

Roger got everyone's respect real quickly as he pitched a perfect three innings to lead the AL to a 3–2 win. Roger wound up as the winning pitcher and the MVP of the game. Darryl Strawberry, who struck out in his only appearance against Roger, became a believer. "No one in the National League throws as hard as he does."

Roger had pitched sensationally and enjoyed incredible success so far. But he knew he couldn't stop to savor it now; he knew he had to keep his focus on Boston's drive for first place.

After the Red Sox started the second half of the season by dropping two games to the Mariners, Roger came riding to the rescue and picked up his 16th win. Boston dropped its next four games, but Roger stopped the slide with a two-hitter against the Angels. In the space of five days Roger lost two games to the White Sox, the second one 1–0 on his own throwing error. It was the last time he would lose that season. His next game was a no-decision affair, and he followed that with an unartistic win against Detroit and a two-hitter against the Twins for his 19th win.

Roger got to go for number 20 in Texas, against the Rangers. Roger felt good before the game because family and friends had come up to see him and because his wife, Debbie, had given him a puppy as a surprise present. And he felt good during the game. "It was my favorite weather, hot and muggy, and I had good stuff." He also had a two-hitter and a 2–0 lead after seven innings, but he gave up a two-run homer in the eighth and wound up with a disappointing no-decision.

Roger's next shot at number 20 was on August 30, exactly a year after he had had the shoulder surgery. This time he cashed in the chips, beating Cleveland at Fenway. The win also put a break on another Boston mini-slump and sent the Bosox off on an 11-game winning streak that tightened their grip on first place.

Roger also won his next four decisions, which added a final flourish to a sensational season. At 24–4, he had the best record and the most wins in either league; he had the best ERA in the American League and was second in strikeouts; he had won the All-Star Game and its MVP award; he had won 14 straight to start the season; he had set a major-league single-game strikeout record and had been the stopper whenever the Red Sox started to slide. It was an entire career's worth of awesome achievements wrapped into one spectacular season.

And there was more to come.

Roger got the call to open the American League Championship Series against the Angels at Fenway. During the season Roger had won all three of his starts against the Angels, allowing only eight runs (seven earned). But this time he just didn't have it. He gave up as many runs in 7 1/3 innings as he had in 26 innings during the season. As catcher Rich Gedman, the person with the best view, observed, "Roger was throwing the ball right down the middle of the plate. He *never* throws the ball down the middle of the plate."

Roger was given the ball again in the fourth game, with Boston trailing two games to one in the best-of-seven series and needing a win. Roger spun a beautiful game for eight innings and carried a 3–0 lead into the ninth. But Doug DeCinces led off the inning with a line-drive homer, and the game began to unravel. Roger walked the eighth and ninth hitters, Dick Schofield and Bob Boone, after he had both of them down 0–2 in the count. "I made bad, careless pitches. I threw pitches that were too hittable in situations where they had to be swinging [at anything even close to the plate]." McNamara decided to make a change and brought in Calvin Schiraldi, Roger's former Texas teammate, to put out the fire. But Calvin didn't do it. The Angels tied the game in the ninth and won it in the 11th.

But Boston bounced back to even the series at three games each, and Roger was given one more chance—the chance to wrap up the ALCS and put the Red Sox in the World Series.

Roger didn't make any mistakes in this game. He held the Angels to three harmless hits over seven innings, and this time Schiraldi held the lead. "It was a magical year and a great finale," said a very happy Roger Clemens.

And then Roger and the Red Sox were headed to Shea Stadium to meet the Amazing New York Mets in the 1986 World Series.

Roger squared off against Dwight Gooden in game two after Bruce Hurst had won a 1–0 thriller in game one. It was billed as a classic pitching duel between the top two pitchers in baseball. But the matchup never materialized. Boston blasted Gooden for six runs in five innings, and Roger got the hook in the fifth. The Red Sox won the game, 9–3, but Roger wound up with a no-decision for not completing the fifth inning.

Roger got the ball again in the sixth game with the Red Sox leading three games to two and had the opportunity to bring Boston its first World Series championship since 1918.

Roger breezed early, striking out six of the first nine batters and pitching no-hit ball through four innings. The Boston bats supported Roger with single runs in the first and second innings, but he gave both of them back in the fifth. Darryl Strawberry started the rally by drawing a leadoff walk and promptly stealing second. Then Ray Knight broke up the no-hitter by singling Darryl home. Mookie Wilson singled Knight to third, and Knight came in to score the tying run while Danny Heep was grounding into a double play.

The Red Sox regained the lead 3–2 in the top of the seventh, and Roger set the Mets down one-two-three in their turn. In the top of the eighth McNamara made another controversial decision. He decided to pinch-hit for Roger and try to score an insurance run. But Boston didn't get that run, and the Mets came right back and tied the score in the bottom of the eighth. Then they pulled out an amazing victory in the tenth to tie the series at three games each.

Roger soaked his arm in ice for two days, trying to get ready for a relief role in the seventh game. "I still thought this was going to be our year." But the Mets thought otherwise and beat Boston, 8–5.

Losing the World Series was a big disappointment for Roger, but the rewards for his outstanding season were still in front of him. On November 12 it was announced that Roger was the unanimous winner of the Cy Young Award in the American League, and six days later he was named the American League's MVP. Roger was thrilled with the recognition, but as he said, "I'd trade both awards in for the world championship ring."

But the biggest highlight in Roger's year came a few weeks later, when his wife gave birth to a baby boy. They named the baby Koby with a *K* because there had to be a *K* in the name of the son of the man who pitched the 20-K game.

6

King of the Hill

Roger had dozens of opportunities to make appearances around the country and cash in on his fame, but he turned most of them down because he didn't want to take time away from his family or from his conditioning for the upcoming season. "I'm not going to let outside income interfere with my priorities," said Roger.

Roger reported to spring training in good physical condition but without peace of mind because he didn't feel that the Red Sox were offering him a fair contract. After two weeks of fruitless negotiations, Roger walked out of camp. The Red Sox threatened to fine Roger $1,000 per day for every day that he missed camp. Roger's agent responded by saying that they would increase their salary demands by $1,500 a day.

Roger was bringing the same tenacity to the contract squabble that he brought to the pitcher's mound. And as Don Baylor pointed out, that's a lot of tenacity. "Roger has the same temperament Nolan Ryan has on the mound. He has the drive and determination to be the best. He's stubborn and he's not going to back down. If you hit him, you have to earn it. He won't give in to the hitter."

After a month of stalled negotiations Commissioner Peter Ueberroth took the unusual step of getting personally involved. "Because," as a person in his office put it, "he feels that Roger Clemens is an exceptional player and should be in uniform."

Roger got back in uniform and went right out and pitched six innings of no-hit, ten-K ball in an exhibition against Harvard University.

But Roger still wasn't entirely satisfied with the contract details. He felt that too much money was tied up in performance incentives and not enough in guaranteed salary. But he just said, "Give me the ball and put my name down [in the starting rotation]. I might have to take my lumps in the first couple of starts, but I'm ready."

Roger was right. He lost his first two starts of the season. And even though he threw a three-hit shutout against the Royals in his next game, he was finding it difficult to get into his really good rhythm. He was working hard, but he didn't have the sharp edge, the concentration and fluidity that a pitcher needs to be effective. Even as late as mid-June, he had only a 4–6 record and a 3.51 ERA after 13 starts.

But then it clicked into place. All the running and sweating and throwing began to pay off. Roger found his rhythm and went on a roll. He won four straight and 16 of his last 19 decisions, including two season-closing gems—a 13-K shutout of the Yankees in the Stadium and a 12-K, two-hit shutout of the Brewers four days later for his 20th win.

It was a day and season of triumph for Roger, but it was also tinged with bitterness. He resented the fact that he had had to pitch the last game of the season in cold weather and on only three days' rest—thereby risking damage to his arm—in order to win 20 games and the Cy Young Award so that he could earn a $300,000 incentive bonus. "Basically, I had to go out there and earn something that should have been in the contract in the first place. We're twenty games out, and I'm out there pitching meaningless games to try to win some individual awards so I can get paid what I deserve."

In 1987, the year of the hitter, when only one other pitcher—Dave Stewart—was able to notch 20 wins, Roger showed that he had remained king of the hill. He led the league in complete games (18) and shutouts (7) and was second in strikeouts (256) while posting the third-lowest ERA (2.97). Roger's accomplishments were acknowledged with his second Cy Young Award, he became only the fourth pitcher to win the award in consecutive seasons. And he had done it in his first two complete seasons in the majors.

Rocket got off to a flying start in 1988. By the All-Star Game he had a 15–5 record and was leading the majors in shutouts with seven. Without Roger the Red Sox, who were nine games out of first, would have fallen out of sight and out of the race.

The Red Sox were battling injuries and rumors that manager John McNamara was going to be dismissed. But Roger didn't allow himself to get distracted or demoralized. "Everybody wants to win," observed Rich Gedman, "but it burns much deeper in him than it does in other people. That's his edge. It's always like, 'I'll show you.'"

But after the All-Star Game, after the Red Sox *had* changed managers—replacing McNamara with Joe Morgan—and after Roger had pitched a three-hit, 14-K win over Texas on July 25 that capped a 12-game Red Sox winning streak that put them back in the race, the Rocket sputtered. Roger was 0–5 in August, and from July 26 through the end of the season he compiled a 3–7 record with a hefty 4.86 ERA.

Roger had never gone through a streak like this before. It was uncomfortable for him and confusing to everybody else. Just as some people were beginning to whisper that Roger had lost some of the zip on his heater, he seemed to right himself. He won two of his last three decisions, but in a key game against Cleveland in the last week of the season he didn't get the job done. The pitcher who always wanted the ball in the tight situations had come up short. He stopped by manager Joe Morgan's office and, speaking about the American League Championship Series, told him not to worry. "Next time you'll see the real Roger."

But after that Friday night loss in Cleveland, Morgan had to worry that he might have to wait until spring training to see Roger pitch again. And even after Boston backed into first place with only 89 wins, "next time" didn't turn out any better than the last time.

The Red Sox had lost the first game of the ALCS against the Oakland Athletics, and Roger was asked to turn the series around before the Red Sox got swept away. Roger answered the call, but only for six innings. He shut the A's down on just two hits, and after Boston scored two unearned runs in the bottom of the sixth, Joe Morgan was feeling good. "I thought we were a shoo-in. The way he was throwing the ball, I figured no way they do it."

But they did it. Dave Henderson led off the seventh with a single. The next hitter was José Canseco, who had led the majors in home runs and RBIs. Roger got ahead in the count 0–2 and then tried to jam José with a fastball in on the fists. But José got around on the 93-MPH pitch and hit a towering home run over the Green Monster that tied the game at 2–2.

Roger has always felt that a key to be a dominating pitcher is to shut the other team down right after your team scores. It keeps the momentum flowing your way and keeps the other team down. But Roger let the A's get back in the game with Canseco's clout, and then he threw away the lead.

Dave Parker, the next hitter, reached Roger for a single. And after Carney Lansford forced Parker, Roger balked Lansford to second. Roger got the second out of the inning on a line drive but then wild-pitched Lansford to third. Mark McGwire was the next hitter, and Roger tried going after him. He got ahead 0–2 and was one pitch away from limiting the damage. But, McGwire lined a pitch into left field and the A's had the lead, 3–2.

Roger's season ended in that seventh inning, and two games later it ended for the rest of the team as the A's swept the Red Sox, 4–0.

The 1988 season, which had begun with such bright promise, had ended in dark disappointment. There were no awards or post-season championships to celebrate. But even though the season hadn't ended on a high note, it certainly hadn't been a disaster. Roger still won 18 games, led the majors in strikeouts with 291, and tied Orel Hershiser for the most shutouts with eight. And the Red Sox, despite the sweep by the A's, had won the Eastern Division race.

And looking ahead to 1989 and beyond, expect the Rocket to soar again. He has some memorabilia that he wants to meet up with. After the 20-K masterpiece, Roger was asked to part with some items that he used that night, including a game ball, his spikes, and his cap to the Hall of Fame. Roger wants to make sure that he keeps pitching well enough for the Hall of Fame to add his bust to the collection. "For a baseball player, Cooperstown is the only place you want to end up at."

ROGER CLEMENS

Courtesy of the University of Texas

Roger jumps for joy after a Longhorn win.

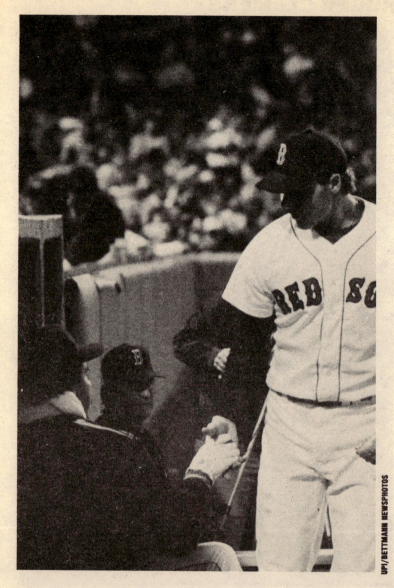

Roger gets his hand shook during his 20K game.

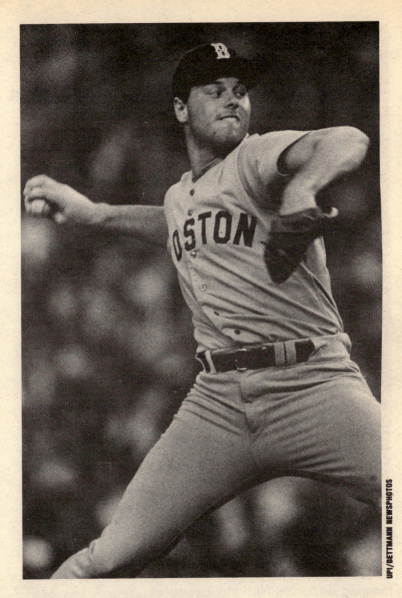

Focusing in against the Yankees.

Mowing down the National Leaguers.

The first pitch of the 1986 ALCS.

Bringing it home against the New York Mets.

DARRYL STRAWBERRY

Darryl takes it downtown.

UPI/BETTMANN

Muscling the ball in batting practice.

Daylight robbery at Wrigley Field.

Darryl blasts a dinger.

Flashing the speed.

Mitchell B. Reibel-SportsChrome

Darryl gets set to strike.

DARRYL STRAWBERRY

1

Baseball Fanatic

Darryl Strawberry was born March 12, 1962, in the city of the Angels, Los Angeles, California. He was the third son in three years for Ruby and Henry Strawberry. And in the next few years, two daughters, Regina and Michelle, came along to complete the Strawberry household.

Darryl fell in love with baseball at a very young age. He was always tagging along with his older brothers, Michael and Ronnie, when they trotted over to John Moseley's house to learn the game. John, who was a baseball coach and a neighbor, had taken the three brothers under his wing. Sometimes he would sit on his stoop and talk baseball to the boys, and sometimes he would take them to a local park and drill them in the fundamentals.

When the workouts were finished and the boys had worked up an appetite, John would often take them to a Jack-in-the-Box for some fast-food delight.

The South Los Angeles neighborhood where they lived was a tough neighborhood, and John cautioned the boys against becoming involved in any street fighting. "Your hands are too important to be using them for punching," he told them. "How," he asked them, "are you gonna play ball with a broken hand?"

But mostly Mr. Moseley talked about baseball and taught the boys how to play. "Everything I know about the game," says Darryl, "I heard it first from him." And John still remembers Darryl's devotion to baseball. "It was all he talked about. Darryl was a baseball fanatic."

Darryl began playing organized baseball when he was nine years old, but in the early going his enthusiasm easily outpaced his ability. He had so much trouble with the bat that the only way he ever got on base was when he bunted.

But it wasn't too long before Darryl began to bang the ball and develop his enormous athletic ability. He was taller and faster and more talented than most of the other kids, and he loved to play ball.

And it was that talent, desire, and good upbringing that allowed Darryl to escape the clutches of the neighborhood gangs. He would tell them that he wasn't interested, that he was going to be a pro ballplayer. "They'd laugh, but they'd leave me alone. I really believed it, though."

He just wasn't sure which sport he was going to be a pro in. But Darryl, a strong-armed, left-handed quarterback, quickly decided that it wouldn't be football. "Football had too much contact, so I knew pretty early that it wasn't for me." But Darryl's talents on the baseball field continued to soar—so much so that his brother, Michael, who was already a star center fielder at Crenshaw High School, told the coach, "When my brother gets to high school, you'll really see something!"

But before Darryl got to strut his stuff at Crenshaw, the Strawberry household suffered a serious blow. Darryl's mom decided to divorce her husband, and the children were left without a father in their home. Ruby, who worked for a phone company, just wouldn't accept the fact that Henry, who was a postal worker, gambled a lot. "I couldn't live like that. We had the house to take care of, the children to take care of, and everything that goes along with it. He played the horses. He wasn't responsible."

Ruby Strawberry is a strong and loving woman and she made certain that the family held together. As Darryl explains it: "Everyone knows about the pressure of the athletic field, but we had to face a different kind of pressure in our own family. Mom made sure that we did it without any problems. The five of us kids grew closer together and closer to Mom."

But despite Ruby's best efforts to create a caring and disciplined home life, divorces do cause pain. And for some reason, the divorce seemed to disturb Darryl more than his brothers and sisters. "It was," admits Darryl, "tough to deal with."

2

Number One

When Darryl finally did get to Crenshaw High School, the baseball coach, Brooks Hurst, was impressed with his ability, but he had problems with Darryl's attitude. Darryl was moody, hard to reach, still hurting from his father's departure. "I think that had a lot to do with it," says Darryl. "We had to go through a lot of bad times. I carried a bad attitude around with me. I believed I didn't have to listen to anyone, didn't have to do anything."

One day Darryl decided that he didn't have to run in from right field. Coach Hurst disagreed. He tapped Darryl's baseball cap and told him, "If you want to wear that C, you've got to hustle." Darryl became angry and yelled, "Nobody touches me." And then he took off his baseball jersey, gave it to Hurst, and just like that quit the team. "I just can't play anymore," he announced.

Darryl later asked the coach to reinstate him, but Hurst refused. He thought he could teach Darryl a useful lesson by keeping him off the team, and the plan worked. "It was the best thing that could have happened to me," says Darryl. "I learned from that situation. I had to be more serious if I wanted to make baseball my career. When I finally understood, I think it made me a better player."

The following season, Darryl's junior year at Crenshaw, he began to blossom as a baseball player. He hit .371 and crashed four home runs and posted a 4–1 record as a hard-throwing part-time pitcher. Darryl and senior Chris Brown, who hit .454, led Crenshaw to the finals of the Los Angeles city championship game, which they lost to Grenada Hills High School, 10–4, at Dodger Stadium. The leading player for Grenada was another right fielder and part-time pitcher by the name of John Elway, who would go on to fame tossing footballs for Stanford University and the Denver Broncos.

It was Chris Brown who drew the scouts to the Crenshaw games, and he didn't disappoint them. But their eyes lit up when they also discovered the lanky left-hander with the rocket arm who uncoiled his body so gracefully and stung the ball so smartly.

In Darryl's senior year he was a starting forward on the Crenshaw H.S. basketball team. They won the city championship and then went up to Oakland for the state championship. When Darryl finally got through with the basketball season, he had only one day to practice baseball before the season opener.

When the Crenshaw team took the field, Darryl was surprised to see that there were dozens of college and major-league scouts in the stands, along with TV cameras and crews to record how the tall, slim stinger would do. "What's going on here?" thought Darryl. "I didn't know I was such a big deal."

Darryl, unnerved by the unexpected attention and uncomfortable at the plate because of his lack of practice, failed to get a hit in his first two trips to the plate. On his third try, though, Darryl came up with the bases loaded and stroked a grand slam. "That was it," said Darryl. "I knew it was baseball season."

Darryl wore his baseball cap everywhere, except at the dinner table. The first time he tried that his mother told him, "Boy, take it off at the table." But as soon as dinner was done, the cap was back on. "It got to the point that my mother thought the cap was a part of my head."

Darryl began thinking about the upcoming major-league baseball draft, especially after *Sports Illustrated* did a feature on him that suggested that he was the number-one prospect in the country. More than one scout compared him in looks and ability to another left-handed-hitting outfielder by the name of Ted Williams. Darryl had never heard of Ted Williams, but he appreciated the compliment when he found out that the former Red Sox slugger had a plaque in the Hall of Fame and was the last major leaguer to hit over .400.

Phil Pote, a former major-league scout who was coaching college baseball in Los Angeles, was among Darryl's many admirers. "He's got bat quickness; he can drive the ball. The ball jumps off his bat. Any swing of his can hurt you. He's just a natural hitter."

It was that hitting ability that allowed Darryl to have some fancy dreams. "I dream about being the number-one draft choice in the nation and being in the major leagues at the age of twenty," he told a reporter.

Actually, though, Darryl was also thinking about accepting a college scholarship from Oklahoma State that would allow him to play both basketball and baseball. Darryl's mother really wanted him to go to college and continue his education, but she had enough confidence in her son to leave the final choice up to him. "It's your future; do what you have to do," she told him.

Darryl decided that if he was one of the top five picks in the baseball draft, he would sign with the pros. He realized that if he was picked, he would need an experienced sports agent to negotiate the best possible deal for him. He finally selected Richie Bry because "He came out to the house and showed he cared about me and my family, not just his own fortunes."

Darryl tried to push the draft out of his mind so that he could concentrate on playing ball. But one day, while Darryl was in a classroom, he was called to the office and found out that the first part of his dream had come true: The New York Mets had made him the number-one pick in the nation. Within a short time Los Angeles television stations had film crews at Crenshaw High to interview the teenage celebrity. But when Number One got home, he was just plain Darryl. Michael and Ronnie weren't excited, because they had been expecting it to happen, and Michelle and Regina couldn't figure out what all the fuss was about. Darryl's mom just said, "Congratulations. Let's eat."

Outside of the Strawberry home, however, there was a lot of excitement. The scouts who had been watching Darryl declared that his potential was unlimited and began comparing him to Hall of Famers before he even signed his contract.

Charlie Fox, a scout for the Expos who had spent a lot of time in the big leagues, said, "I'd give up five of our picks if we could get that kid."

And another scout, Hugh Alexander, said, "He's the best prospect I've seen in the last thirty years."

Darryl was floating about ten feet off the ground. "Back then all I could think about was playing baseball for the New York Mets." But he came down to earth long enough to finish the season with a .400 average and five dingers. Then he signed a contract that called for a $200,000 signing bonus, and he was on his way.

3

Turkey Neck

Darryl, who was eighteen years old and who had been out of the state of California only once in his life, was assigned to the Mets' Rookie League team in faraway Kingsport, Tennessee.

When Darryl arrived in Kingsport, the first person whom he met was Chuck Hiller, his new manager. If Darryl was expecting any special treatment or a warm welcome, Hiller quickly popped that bubble. "So, you're the new turkey neck they're sending me. Well, work hard, turkey neck. If you work hard, you can make it to the bigs."

Darryl didn't adjust easily to being alone and away from home for the first time. "The change in my life wasn't easy. I wanted to make the best of it, but I'll admit I was homesick. I called my mother almost every night. She tried to keep my spirits up, but it was tough."

It was also difficult for Darryl's mom. "He sounded so pitiful. He was lost. I'd try to talk chipper, telling him, 'Now look, you can't be like that.' And then I'd get the phone bill and nearly faint. I told him that he was going to spend all his money on those phone calls."

In between bouts of homesickness Darryl did manage to play 44 games. He hit .268 with five homers and 20 RBIs while striking out 39 times—not exactly all-star numbers. "Hardly anything special," acknowledges Darryl.

Darryl even wondered if he had made a mistake in not accepting the college scholarship and the chance to develop as a basketball player. But he worked on thinking positively and building up his confidence during the winter. By the time he left for spring training, Darryl was confident that he'd pick up the pace.

Darryl, who was assigned to Lynchburg (Virginia) in the Class A Carolina League, got off to a horrible start. By July he had *raised* his average to an anemic .221. The pressure to produce began to build on Darryl. He was keenly aware of the fact that he wasn't living up to anyone's expectations. And just in case he needed help in figuring it out, the Lynchburg fans weren't shy about expressing their disappointment. Pretty soon Darryl was reading stories in the local papers suggesting that the Mets had wasted their number-one pick. The booing and the negative stories further eroded Darryl's confidence. He was only nineteen and extremely sensitive, and he began to doubt his own abilities.

Darryl was hurt and confused, and decided that he was going to throw in the towel and head back to Los Angeles. Before he left, Gene Dusan, the Lynchburg manager, sat Darryl for a marathon rap session. Dusan told Darryl that he had a down world of talent and that no one in the Mets' organization had given up on him. "Don't give up on yourself," he told Darryl. "Stop reading the sports pages and listening to the sportscasters. They have their jobs to do and you have yours. And don't worry about the fans. Their boos will turn to cheers as soon as you start to stroke the ball. Don't let other people run you out of the game."

The next day Darryl was back in the lineup. "It took a lot of doing, but I'm sure glad that Gene got me to go back." Darryl rewarded Dusan's faith by closing out the season strongly. He brought his average up to .255 and hit thirteen homers while knocking in 78 runs and swiping 31 bases.

Darryl still hadn't produced like a "phenom," but that season at Lynchburg marked a turning point in Darryl's development as a player and as a person. "I was finally maturing," recalls Darryl. "Whenever I have problems now, I look back at Lynchburg and remember how immature I was and how close I came to quitting. I knew it would never happen again."

Darryl hoped that he had put all his doubts and troubles behind him. It seemed as though his young career had been derailed, and he was anxious to get it back on the fast track, so when Darryl went home after the season he worked out on a regular basis to keep himself in shape. And the Mets showed their faith in Darryl by promoting him to their Jackson (Mississippi) club in the Class AA Texas League.

Darryl began the season with a bang and kept right on blasting. He hit for the cycle (single, double, triple, and home run) on opening day and continued his rampage for the entire season. He finished with a league-leading 34 homers, drove in 97 runs, hit .283, stole 45 bases, and drew 100 walks from pitchers who preferred to see Darryl standing on first base than to watch him circling the bases in his familiar home-run trot.

Darryl, who was chosen as the Most Valuable Player in the Texas League, had finally put together the kind of season that everyone had been expecting from him. But before Darryl had the chance to savor his success, he was promoted to the Mets' Triple A team in Tidewater (Virginia). He went five for 20 and helped the Tides win the International League play-offs.

Darryl went home to Los Angeles feeling as though he were on top of the world. But after a short round of celebrations, Darryl was back working out, harder and earlier than ever before. "Most of my friends couldn't understand that. They wanted to know why I was working out in November. Nobody understood how dedicated I could be, but I was determined to show them. I was only one step away from the majors."

What helped to fuel Darryl's dedication was the fact that

he had been invited to go to spring training with the Mets. So when February rolled around, Darryl packed his bags and took off for St. Petersburg, Florida, and his first major-league training camp.

Darryl was excited and hopeful, but also nervous and doubtful that the Mets would jump him directly from Double A to the majors without a season of experience at the Triple A level. But he took advantage of his opportunity to impress the Mets' management by leading the team in hitting and winning the Johnny Murphy award as the top rookie in the Mets camp.

Darryl was hoping that his performance would earn him an opening-day appearance at Shea Stadium. But Frank Cashen, the general manager of the Mets, decided that Darryl would be better off getting some more seasoning in the minors. Cashen didn't want to rush Darryl and then see him wilt in the heat of the major-league spotlight. He had seen too many promising players have their careers shattered because they were brought up to the big leagues before they could handle the pitching or the pressure.

Darryl was disappointed when he was given the news, but he was told that, if he stroked the ball at Tidewater like he had in spring training, he would be called up before the All-Star Game. After just sixteen games, with Darryl sailing along at a .333 clip, the call came. The first thing that Darryl did after getting the good news from Davey Johnson, who was the manager at Tidewater, was to call home and share it with his family. Then he boarded the gray metal bird and was on his way to the Big Apple.

4

Rookie

The 1983 Mets were not a good team, and they had gotten off to a slow start. At 6–15, they were threatening to go into reverse and quickly disappear into last-place oblivion. The Met fans and the reporters who covered the team were hungry for a winner and a star to root for. They were hoping that Darryl would be an instant star and put some pop into the lineup and get the team moving forward. Darryl realized the situation and was uncomfortable with it. He just wanted to concentrate on breaking into a major-league lineup. He didn't want to feel like he had the responsibility of carrying the team on his back.

Frank Cashen and George Bamberger, the Mets' manager, didn't want any extra pressure put on Darryl either. They knew that young players usually need a period of adjustment to the majors before they can play up to their potential. Most rookies are realizing a lifetime dream. They are suddenly playing with and against players they have watched on TV and idolized. A few years earlier they were collecting the bubble-gum cards of players they're now standing on the same field with. It can be mind blowing.

And the stadiums are so much bigger and filled with so many more people than they're used to. And those people are expecting results. "This is the major leagues, kid. Play like a major leaguer." For a lot of rookies their lives have been one-way express trips to the top. They may have suffered some slumps, but for the most part they've always been the star, the engine driving their teams. Their careers have always gone in one direction—up. Now they're at the top of the mountain, and while it's a dream come true, the view can be dizzying. They wonder if they're really good enough, or if their dream will turn into a nightmare and send them tumbling down that slippery mountain.

The fans and the press, and even teammates and management, can create a lot of pressure because of their hopes and expectations. And the brighter the prospect, the higher the expectations, especially when the rest of the team is floundering and there's no one else to root for or pin hopes on. And it had been a long time since anyone had generated as much anticipation as Darryl. He had been the number-one pick in the country and saddled with a "can't miss" tag since high school. He had been compared to Ted Williams since he was a teenager. Darryl had all the tools that scouts look for—he could hit, hit for power, run, catch, and throw—but he had never been tested on a major-league field against major-league pitching.

Major-league pitchers, most of the time, are levels above the best pitcher whom a rookie has ever faced. They throw harder, have better breaking pitches, change speeds more effectively, and have better control of their pitches—and they're smarter. They know how to work a hitter and probe his weak spots.

When the Mets' management called a press conference to introduce Darryl to the New York media and through them to the Mets' fans, they were aware of all the pressure that Darryl was about to face, and they did their best to ease it. They made it clear that they didn't expect Darryl to carry the team or achieve instant stardom. But everyone knew that they were really hoping he would do both. And Darryl tried to be cool, and said that he didn't feel any pressure. But his mother, who was at the press conference, knew otherwise. "I know my son. I could see the strain in Darryl's face, and I know he felt the pressure. People were always comparing him to somebody."

Darryl's first appearance in a major-league lineup came against the Cincinnati Reds and their ace, Mario Soto. The crowd at Shea Stadium cheered when Darryl took his place in the batter's box, hoping that the tall, good-looking rookie would tag one. But Soto threw Darryl three straight change-ups, and Darryl was back in the dugout without ever having touched the ball. Darryl also struck out his next two times up and ended up going zero for four against Soto. After the Reds' ace left the game, Darryl got on base twice with walks, stole a base, and even scored the winning run when George Foster hit a three-run homer in the 13th inning. But it had not been a star-spangled beginning for the young slugger. Or as Darryl put it: "I never saw that kind of stuff in the minor leagues."

Darryl went 0 for 11 before he got his first hit, a run-scoring single to left field. A week later, on May 16, he stroked his first major-league home run. "That was a special feeling. I figured I had found myself and things were going to be okay." The next day Darryl hit another homer, a three-run blast off Tim Lollar that powered the Mets to a 6–4 win over the San Diego Padres.

But Darryl soon showed that he wasn't much of a prophet, because a few weeks later he was hitting a microscopic .161 with only three homers and nine RBIs, and nothing was okay. Darryl was struggling at the plate and embarrassed at his lack of production. Darryl, the kid with the sweet swing, had taken a nosedive. Not only wasn't he carrying his share of the load, he wasn't even hitting his weight. He wasn't rapping the ball against right-handers, and left-handers were making him look foolish. They were jamming him with inside fastballs and then coming back with curveballs low and away that either froze Darryl into inaction or produced feeble swings like a barn door flapping in the wind.

"It was," says Darryl, "the most difficult time of my life.

I tried too much to pressure myself to hit home runs, to show people what I could do. I was suddenly in the majors with all those guys I'd been watching for years, and now I didn't know where I fit in."

Just when Darryl felt that he was drowning, Jim Frey, the Mets' hitting instructor, threw him a lifeline. "I didn't know which way to turn, and then Frey stepped in like a father and said, 'I'm going to help you, but you've got to help yourself.'"

Frey knew that he had to get Darryl to want to work harder and to be more aggressive at the plate. But his main job was to help Darryl rebuild his confidence before it got sucked into a black hole and disappeared.

Frey did his work well, and Darryl began to belt the ball. By the end of the season he had raised his batting average to .257 while setting Met rookie records with 26 home runs and 74 RBIs. Darryl's freshman campaign had started off on a sour note, but he ended it on a high note by being named the National League's Rookie of the Year.

5

Great Expectations

Darryl went to spring training in 1984 feeling that his life and career were running as smoothly as a ten-speed racer down a newly paved road. During the off-season he had met a woman named Lisa, and they had fallen in love. And Darryl had also made contact with his father. "It was important to me that we come together again. It was difficult, though, because I had to fight the feeling of not wanting to include him in my life. Mom helped me to overcome that feeling." And on the baseball front, observers were predicting greatness. Frank Howard, who had managed the Mets for most of the 1983 season and had been a big-league slugger himself, summed up the thinking. "He can go as far in baseball as any man living." According to Darryl, "I felt like nothing could go wrong."

The peace was shattered, though, when an article appeared that quoted Darryl as saying that he might have to assume the leadership of the Mets: "I'd always been on ballclubs where the players had the attitude of winning. With the Mets, it sometimes didn't seem to make a difference to certain players. We need someone to bring out a better attitude. What I feel this team needs is a playing leader, and if nobody wants the job, I'll have to take it."

A lot of the veteran players thought that Darryl was off base, and they jumped all over him. They didn't think that he had been on the team long enough or produced enough to be a team leader. Keith Hernandez, the Mets' first baseman and a person that Darryl "really looks up to," finally stepped in, though, and brought the situation under control.

Opening day found the Mets at Cincinnati's Three

Rivers Stadium, and on the mound for the Reds was Darryl's nemesis, Mario Soto. Darryl came to the plate remembering how Soto had embarrassed him in their last meeting, and was determined to do some damage this time.

Soto threw a change-up out of the strike zone that Darryl chased for strike one. He stepped out of the batter's box and told himself to relax. "I was too excited." Darryl took another change-up for a ball. Soto came right back with another change-up, but this time he got the pitch up and in the strike zone. Darryl waited on the pitch and then uncoiled his bat like a cobra striking, and sent the ball on a rising arc into the second tier in right field, 450 feet away from home plate. As Darryl rounded the bases, he felt very content.

Darryl continued to tattoo the ball early in the season. After 22 games, he was hitting .363 with five home runs and thirteen RBIs. But then Darryl sputtered, and the good start soon turned bad and quickly got worse.

Reporters were writing negative stories, the fans at Shea were booing, and some of Darryl's teammates were criticizing his play. Darryl, feeling frustrated and unwanted, went into a funk. "It got so bad, I didn't even feel like playing." One day Darryl showed up so late that he missed batting practice. Davey Johnson, who had become the Mets' manager, fined Darryl and then suggested that he might benefit from a day off. Johnson was surprised when Darryl told him that he wanted more time to think things over. Ballplayers aren't usually given vacations in the middle of a pennant race, but both men thought that it might be better to let Darryl sit on the bench and try to get back on track.

Darryl sat stewing for three games, until Bill Robinson, the Mets' new hitting instructor, got through to Darryl. "He said I wasn't doing the team or myself any good by not playing." He was right.

Darryl came back and began hitting the ball and playing

like the Mets had hoped he would. But in August, Darryl went into another slump (he failed to hit a single home run) and another funk. Keith Hernandez told Darryl that he had quit on himself and was letting the team down. "The talk," said Darryl, "woke me up." But the wake-up call came too late in the season for the Mets to overtake the Chicago Cubs.

The highlight of the season for Darryl was his surprising selection by the fans to a starting berth on the National League All-Star team. And he did manage to post decent stats: a .251 average, 26 homers, 97 RBIs, and 27 stolen bases. But the season that had begun with such promise was essentially a downer. Darryl had shown flashes of brilliance, but he hadn't demonstrated staying power—the ability to take the hard knocks and the slumps, and play through the criticism and the three-and-two curveballs.

Instead of building on his Rookie of the Year performance, Darryl had slipped sideways. As Darryl acknowledged, "It was another learning experience, although I felt I had had enough of those. So much was expected of me, and I expected so much more of myself. I knew eventually it would all show, but after that season I couldn't help but wonder when."

Darryl had great expectations coming into the 1985 season. He and Lisa had gotten married in January, and in March the Mets had made Darryl a millionaire when they gave him one of the best contracts ever given to a third-year player. "This is the best birthday present I've ever received," said Darryl with a smile. "I'll earn it every day I play."

Darryl had wanted to get off quickly, but instead he slumped. He hung in, though, and didn't get down on himself. "I was sure it was just going to be a matter of time before I busted out." But instead of busting out, Darryl tore ligaments in his thumb while making a diving catch of a slicing line drive off the bat of Juan Samuel.

Darryl tried to spend his seven weeks on the bench productively by studying how the better players produced. "The main thing I learned was to be a more disciplined hitter. I watched Keith a lot. He's one of the best hitters in the game, especially as a left-handed hitter against a left-handed pitcher. I saw how he went with the pitch and hit it to all fields. I went over and over in my mind how I would work on doing that when I came back."

When Darryl returned to the lineup, though, his average dipped below .200, and the Mets fell to fourth place. But after Bill Robinson helped Darryl with his batting stance, Darryl began to hit and the Mets began to win. At the All-Star break, they were only two and a half games behind the Cardinals and closing fast.

Despite Darryl's lack of playing time and his sub-star stats, the fans again voted him to the National League All-Star team. A lot of people didn't think Darryl really deserved the spot, and he thought about not playing. "But Gary Carter, among others, convinced me to go, saying the fans voted for me because they wanted to see me, and I never wanted to disappoint my fans." In the game Darryl more than held his own, as he got a hit, stole a base, and scored two runs.

And after the All-Star Game, Darryl began to seriously sting the ball. In a game against the Braves he blasted two home runs, including a grand slam, and knocked in seven runs. On August 5, Darryl hammered three homers against the Cubs, and the Mets slipped past St. Louis into first place.

Going into the last week of the season, the Mets, who had continued to play well, trailed the Cards, who had played even better, by three games. The New Yorkers came into St. Louis for a three-game series, needing a sweep. The first game was scoreless through ten innings, and then, in the 11th, Darryl teed off on a Ken Dayley fastball and sent a screaming line drive 440 feet over the fence and off the clock in right center to buy the Mets some time and the game 1–0. The Mets took the next game too, to shave the Cards' lead to one game. But they ran out of magic and dropped the third game and had to settle for second place.

Darryl had closed with a rush, getting his average up to .277 while whacking 29 home runs, driving in 79 runs, and stealing 26 bases. Darryl and a lot of other people couldn't help thinking that if it hadn't been for his injury, the Mets would have wound up in first place.

Darryl worked hard during the off-season so that he would be ready to spark the Mets in 1986. He also took time to spend with his son, Darryl, Jr. "He's a big part of my life. I want to make him proud of me." Darryl also took the time to become involved with helping others. "I get paid a pretty good salary. A lot of people did a lot of good things for me when I was growing up. In my own way I want to reciprocate and make it easier for other kids to get the opportunity to accomplish things too."

The one thing that Darryl wanted most to accomplish was to lead the Mets to a World Series win. And a lot of experts thought he was primed to do it. Frank Cashen, the Mets' general manager, who has been around a long time and seen lots of great ballplayers, said, "Darryl stands above everyone else. I don't think I've ever come across anyone else with that kind of potential." Tim McCarver, who announces the Mets games and was a first-rate catcher for the Cards and Phillies, thought Darryl could explode. "Nobody knows what Darryl is capable of doing. He hit 29 home runs last year when he missed seven weeks. He could hit *twice* as many this year. He is the one player on the team, maybe in baseball, who could double his numbers."

"But my goal isn't numbers," said Darryl. "I've got a chance to help the Mets reach the only goal that counts in baseball: winning."

The Mets took the first step toward that goal by taking

the Eastern Division, and they didn't just win: They dominated, winning 108 games and beating out the second-place Phillies by 21 1/2 games.

Darryl made a contribution, but he wasn't the spark that lit the fuse. And despite his annual selection to the All-Star team, making him the first National Leaguer ever to be selected as a starter in his first three complete seasons, he didn't put up all-star numbers. His batting average dropped to .259, and he hit only 27 home runs. He also experienced his usual August fade, going 0 for 47 at Shea Stadium during the month.

Darryl still hadn't developed the consistency or put up the numbers of a superstar. Even Darryl acknowledged that his season had "had its ups and downs." The fans at Shea took out their disappointment at his lack of production and his sometimes sloppy play by booing him, which confused Darryl. "We're up by twenty games and I got to take the heat. I don't understand it."

What Darryl didn't understand was that people were growing frustrated waiting for him to live up to his elusive potential and to expend full effort on every play. Even batting coach Bill Robinson began to express impatience and concern. "He has mental lapses at times, and he has times when he doesn't go one hundred percent. Just young mistakes, but young mistakes to a point where you say, 'Hey, this is his fourth year in the major leagues.' What I pray is that five years from now I'm not saying, 'This is the year he can put the numbers on the board.'"

In the National League Championship Series against Houston, which the Mets won four games to two, Darryl didn't hit often (he struck out 12 times in 22 at bats), but he hit when it counted. In game three he hit a tremendous three-run blast off lefty Bob Knepper that tied the score at 4–4. In game five he broke up a Nolan Ryan no-hitter and tied the score at 1–1 when he blasted a fifth-inning home run. The Mets went on to win both of those games. And in the 16th inning of the sixth and final game, he doubled to ignite the winning rally.

In the World Series the Mets fell behind the Red Sox three games to two, and they were down to their last strike of the season *three times* in the tenth inning before pulling out an improbable and stunning victory with a dramatic three-run rally. The Mets burst off the bench and jumped for joy. An excited Keith Hernandez yelled, "It's one of the greatest comebacks in the history of baseball." But Darryl wasn't there to share the joy with his teammates. Darryl, who was batting .200 in the World Series, had been taken out of the game after he made the final out of the eighth inning. Instead of sitting in the dugout and cheering his teammates on, Darryl had stalked into the clubhouse. And when the Mets' celebration reached the clubhouse, Darryl just sat by himself and sulked.

Darryl was shocked and embarrassed and wouldn't even talk to manager Davey Johnson. "I don't have anything to say to him." Johnson, though, remained calm. "Darryl's only thinking of the moment, but it's my job to think an inning or two ahead. It was a move that had to be made."

It was not one of Darryl's finest moments, but fortunately for him he was able to end the season on a happy note. Prior to the seventh game he acknowledged that he had acted badly, and then went out and hit a towering home run in the eighth inning that stretched the Mets' lead to 7–5 on their way to an 8–5 win in the decisive game.

"I struggled throughout the Series," Darryl acknowledged. "To go out with a big hit like that made me happy. I would have been hard on myself. I didn't have the Series I should have. I feel just as badly as the fans do when I don't produce, but I'll get over it and I'll make them love me eventually."

6

A New Beginning

During the off-season Darryl's wife, Lisa, filed for divorce. Darryl, to whom family is so important, was devastated.

And then in spring training Darryl added to his problems by showing up three hours late for a practice. Davey Johnson fined him. Some of his teammates, who were trying to concentrate on getting ready for the season, openly expressed their annoyance. "He overslept?" growled Gary Carter. "Can't he afford an alarm clock?" And Lee Mazzilli voiced the frustration of a lot of people. "He has more talent than anybody in this clubhouse. He has Hall of Fame written all over him. It's time for him to really wake up."

Darryl was apologetic and didn't want to let the incident interfere with his preparation for the season. "I'll put this behind me. I'm not going to let it affect my play. I'm a little upset, but I know I gotta forget about it and play ball this year."

Darryl did just that in the first inning on opening day of 1987 when he crashed a towering three-run homer that powered the Mets to a 3–2 win over the Pittsburgh Pirates.

After the game he announced that he was dedicating his season to his son, Darryl, Jr., and his teammate Dwight Gooden. Darryl, along with the rest of the Mets, had been shocked a week earlier to learn that Dwight had used cocaine and would be starting his season in a rehabilitation center instead of on the mound. "I'm very close to Dwight. He had so much going for him, and yet you can see how your life can be destroyed overnight. It woke me up." Darryl was very definite when he was asked if he used drugs. "I stay away from that stuff. Look at me. I'm six foot six. That's high enough."

Darryl was dealing with serious problems, but he spoke strongly and optimistically. "It's a new year and a new attitude. You've got to believe in new dreams. I want to do well and have fun."

After the first month of the season Darryl, who had opened the season with a ten-game hitting streak, was doing just that. He had hammered seven home runs, hung up 21 RBIs, and was hitting .322. He was hustling and optimistic. "This is going to be my year. I'm relaxed, confident. I know what I can do, how good I can be."

And Darryl was not allowing his personal pain to interfere with his performance, as he had in the past. "There were weeks when I was having the problems at home last season, and I just couldn't concentrate at the park. It's still tough. There's a lot of anger and hurt when you lose a family. I still love and care for them."

The change in Darryl's attitude and performance was dramatic, and Keith Hernandez, for one, noticed the difference. "Darryl's come to play hard. We all have days when we don't feel good. Darryl would give in to them in the past. Now he isn't. He's been great and that's growth."

But in June, Darryl began turning his dream season into a nightmare. Early in the month he reported late for batting practice on two consecutive days, and Davey Johnson fined him and benched him for two days. A week later Darryl was hit by a pitch thrown by Al Nipper and then was tossed out of the game when he ran out to the mound to attack the pitcher. Two weeks after that incident Darryl claimed that he was too sick to play the first two games of an important three-game series against the first-place Cardinals.

Darryl's absences provoked an angry public debate between Darryl and a number of his teammates. Lee

Mazzilli, who replaced Darryl in the lineup, fired the first salvo. "What he did let his manager down, let his coaches down, and, most importantly, let his teammates down."

Darryl was stung by the criticism. "I don't know why they always want to say things about me. I'm sick. I didn't even think of playing. It would only have hurt the club." Mazzilli snapped right back. "A seventy-percent Strawberry is better than a hundred-percent Mazzilli."

"Where would this team be without me?" asked Darryl.

The next day as he expressed the anger that he felt toward Mazzilli, second baseman Wally Backman—another outspoken critic—and the Mets in general, he said, "So I miss a couple of games. When I'm gone from here, they'll wonder why I left."

Darryl often retreats into the dream of leaving New York and returning to Los Angeles to play for the Dodgers. He seems to imagine that the expectations of the fans, the media, and his teammates would somehow be diminished in Los Angeles. It seems as though Darryl would like to re-create an earlier, more secure time in his life, a pressure-free time when his team always won and Darryl was always the star. A time when he played on his own terms, without discipline and without fans to boo him, media people to criticize his lapses, or teammates to challenge him. In the fondest version of this dream, he is joined on the Dodgers by Eric Davis, the star center fielder of the Cincinnati Reds, with whom Darryl played in a Babe Ruth League.

Keith Hernandez, speaking, it seemed, more in sorrow than anger, tried to put the situation in perspective. "The crux of this is that it's been going on for years, and patience has run out with some guys. We need him, but we never know what side of the bed he's going to wake up on."

Then Davey Johnson held a meeting to clear the air. "Into every life a little rain must fall, but you don't want a thunderstorm," he half joked.

A few weeks after that incident Darryl made his fourth consecutive appearance in the starting lineup of the All-Star Game, and a few days after that, on July 20, Davey Johnson made a decision to put Darryl in the cleanup spot in the batting order on a permanent basis.

Being the cleanup hitter was a role that Darryl had always craved, feeling that it would legitimatize his position as the team's dominant hitter. Darryl responded in high style to being put in the number-four spot. He went on a nine-game hitting streak and hit safely in seventeen of twenty games, clouting seven home runs and scoring nineteen runs while bagging fifteen RBIs. He tailed off in the second half of August, but was sensational in September and was named the National League Player of the Month. In the 27 games that Darryl played in September, he hit .317, cracked eight home runs, knocked in 27 runs, scored 24 times, and stole 11 bases. For the season Darryl hit .284, poled 39 home runs, drove in 104 runs, scored 108, stole 36 bases, and drew 97 bases on balls. He entered the very exclusive 30–30 club (thirty homers and thirty stolen bases in the same season). Mets third baseman Howard Johnson also did it, and they became the first pair of teammates ever to go 30–30 in the same year.

Despite Darryl's late-season heroics, the Mets just missed catching the Cardinals. But his second-half performance finally produced the kind of numbers that everyone, including Darryl, had been waiting for. And everyone seemed to agree that Darryl's attitude had soared as high as his performance. Darryl had finally seemed to attain the maturity to go with his talent. "You have to learn. My career is just starting, really."

Darryl's life hit another high note in the off-season when he and Lisa reconciled and they and Darryl, Jr., began living together again. Darryl's life was coming together the way he had always hoped it would.

Darryl felt great and couldn't wait for the 1988 season to begin. He spent a lot of time working out at Shea Stadium and looking forward to leading the Mets back to first place and building on his own accomplishments. "Last year I had a decent season for the first time in my life, and now everything I wanted is within reach." And Darryl showed how much he had grown when he realized, "Sometimes it's good that I've been criticized, even if I didn't act that way at the time. Maybe it did take me longer than people thought it would, but starting now I'm all business. The only time you'll hear from me this season will be because of my bat."

Darryl started the 1988 season in style, going four for four and clouting two massive home runs on opening day in Montreal. The first one easily cleared the center-field fence in Olympic Stadium, landing well over 400 feet from home plate. The second one jumped off the bat like a rocket from a launching pad and struck a track of lights hanging from the retractable roof, about 160 feet off the ground. Everyone in the stadium was stunned. "It was the longest home run I ever saw," marveled Davey Johnson. "Longer than any I saw playing with Frank Robinson or Hank Aaron or Sadaharu Oh in Japan." Darryl was in impressive company: Robinson was number four on the major-league home-run list with 586, Aaron was the major-league champ with 755, and Oh, of the Japanese league, hit more homers than any other pro player in history. It was such an awesome drive that the Expos brought in scientists to determine just how far the ball would have gone if it hadn't hit the light. They estimated that it would have traveled a mind-boggling 545 feet. Tim Teufel thought that it would have gone even farther. The Met infielder was amazed. "I look at home runs like that and I can't even relate to them."

Darryl seemed to be the only one who wasn't excited. "I

don't care how far they go. A home run counts as one run."
But Lee Mazzilli, for one, isn't so casual about Darryl's
at bats. "Whenever Darryl comes to the plate, I make sure
I'm in the dugout. I want to be there the day he hits the
six-hundred-foot home run."

Darryl kept right on blasting home runs, stroking the key
hits, and driving in the big runs. In the early months of
the season, while Keith Hernandez was out for 57 games and
the other Met hitters went into an unexpected hiberna-
tion, Darryl carried the offense, and he powered the team
into first place. As center fielder Mookie Wilson noted,
"There was a lot of pressure this season. For weeks when
Keith was out and Gary [Carter] wasn't hitting, Straw was
our whole offense. If we scored two runs it was because
Darryl hit a two-run homer. If we scored three runs, it was
because Darryl hit a three-run homer."

When Darryl is hot he demoralizes the other teams. Like
Lawrence Taylor of the football Giants, he takes teams out
of their game. He causes managers to throw out the book
and change their fundamental thinking. In the late innings
of tied games managers will consistently walk Darryl in-
tentionally, even though it's always been a cardinal
rule in baseball that you don't put the potential winning run
on base. More than one manager ordered Darryl walked even
though the Mets already had a runner at first. When Jim
Leyland, the manager of the Pirates, was asked why he
would put the potential winning run in scoring position, he
answered with words that became a chorus among National
League managers. "I'm not going to get beat by Darryl
Strawberry. I'll take my chances with the next guy." Pretty
impressive when you realize that the "next guy" in the
Mets' lineup was Kevin McReynolds.

Darryl had finally put all the pieces of the puzzle
together. "Darryl has grown up," observed teammate

Wally Backman. "He's shown me something this year." And Keith Hernandez, who has always been the inspirational leader of the Mets, also noted, "Baseball is a game of perseverance, of not giving in. In the past Darryl didn't have that toughness. He certainly has developed it, though. He will take over the leadership of this team one day. And take it over deservedly."

And Bill Robinson observed that Darryl had finally achieved that quality of intelligent aggressiveness that all great hitters have—the quality that Jim Frey had talked to Darryl about in his rookie year. "In the past, when Darryl had an 0–2 count, you could just see Darryl's face. It said, 'Oh, what am I going to do now?' Today it's 'What can I do to attack the pitch?' That's patience, that's confidence."

Darryl smiled at the turn of events. "I've learned all over again that what it takes to be successful is to be relaxed and confident. When I go out there with a relaxed mind, everything else falls into place. That's basically the way it was for me as a kid. We had so much fun because we were relaxed about what we were doing. Since the second half of last year I've learned to feel that way again. When they put me in the fourth spot, everything clicked. I was sitting where I always wanted to sit."

Darryl, as usual, was voted to the All-Star Game in July, and almost as predictably he went through a slump in August. But Darryl broke out of his slump after Labor Day and helped propel the Mets to their second NL East title in three years. Darryl ended the season the way he had begun it, by blasting two tremendous home runs, which gave him a league-leading 39 and the Mets their 100th victory.

Darryl stayed hot and lit a spark for the Mets in the opening play-off game against the Los Angeles Dodgers. The Mets were trailing 2–0 in the ninth inning when Darryl lined a double off Orel Hershiser. The hit drove in

Greg Jefferies with the first run scored off Hershiser in a record-setting 67 innings and ignited a three-run rally that gave the Mets a dramatic come-from-behind win.

Darryl had a strong series against the Dodgers, including a three-for-five, three-RBI performance in game three and a two-run homer in game four. But the Mets kept slipping and the Dodgers kept winning. And as Darryl said after the Mets had lost the fifth game, "When you keep playing catch-up, eventually it catches up." It finally caught up to the Mets when Hershiser shut them out in the seventh and final game.

It was an agonizing loss for the Mets, particularly because they had beaten the Dodgers ten out of 11 games in the regular season and were heavily favored in the play-offs. Darryl spoke for the entire team when he said, "We should have won it in five games. We beat ourselves. Now we have to live with it. The fans in New York love us and support us all year. This is a heartache for us and for them. We're sorry."

Darryl suffered another disappointment when Kirk Gibson, the Dodgers' left fielder, beat him out in the voting for the National League's Most Valuable Player award. But Darryl, who had posted much better numbers than Gibson, accepted the decision gracefully. "I'm not really disappointed," said Darryl, trying to hide his disappointment. "Gibson had a great year. I was important to my team, and that's the important thing. I wasn't overlooked; I finished second. I'm not down. Life goes on. I'm a happy man. I've got a beautiful wife and two beautiful kids." And then he laid down a challenge for himself. "I think expectation is the byword. People really expect an all-around performance from me, which they will get in 1989."

ROGER CLEMENS

YEAR	CLUB	W-L	ERA	G	GS	CG	SHO	SV	IP	H	R	ER	BB	SO
1983	Winter Haven	3–1	1.24	4	4	3	1	0	29.0	22	4	4	0	36
	New Britain	4–1	1.38	7	7	3	1	0	52.0	31	8	8	12	59
1984	Pawtucket	2–3	1.93	7	6	3	1	0	46.2	39	12	10	14	50
	Boston - a	9–4	4.32	21	20	5	1	0	133.1	146	67	64	29	126
1985	Boston - b,c	7–5	3.29	15	15	3	1	0	98.1	83	38	36	37	74
1986	Boston	24–4	2.48	33	33	10	1	0	254.0	179	77	70	67	238
1987	Boston	20–9	2.97	36	36	18	7	0	281.2	248	100	93	83	256
1988	Boston	18–12	2.93	35	35	14	8	0	264.0	217	93	86	62	291
Major League Totals		78–34	3.04	140	139	50	18	0	1031.1	873	375	349	278	985

a. Injured right forearm August 31, 1984, and sidelined for rest of season.
b. On Disabled List with sore right shoulder July 8 to August 3, 1985.
c. On Disabled List with sore right shoulder August 21 for rest of season; had operation August 30, 1985.

CHAMPIONSHIP SERIES RECORD

YEAR	CLUB	W-L	ERA	G	GS	CG	SHO	SV	IP	H	R	ER	BB	SO
1986	Boston vs. Cal.	1–1	4.37	3	3	0	0	0	22.2	22	12	11	7	17
1988	Boston vs. Oak.	0–0	3.86	1	1	0	0	0	7.0	6	3	3	0	8

WORLD SERIES

YEAR	CLUB	W-L	ERA	G	GS	CG	SHO	SV	IP	H	R	ER	BB	SO
1986	Boston vs. Mets	0–0	3.18	2	2	0	0	0	11.1	9	5	4	6	11

ALL-STAR GAME RECORD

YEAR	LEAGUE	POS	W-L	ERA	IP	H	R	ER	BB	SO
1986	A.L., Boston	P	1–0	0.00	3	0	0	0	0	2
1988	A.L., Boston	P	0–0	0.00	1	0	0	0	0	2

DARRYL STRAWBERRY

YEAR	CLUB	AVG.	G	AB	R	H	2B	3B	HR	RBI	BB	SO	SB
1980	Kingsport (Rookie)	.268	44	157	27	42	5	2	5	20	20	39	5
1981	Lynchburg (A)	.255	123	420	84	107	22	6	13	78	82	105	31
1982	Jackson (AA)	.283	129	435	93	123	19	9	34	97	100	145	45
1983	Tidewater (AAA)	.333	16	57	12	19	4	1	3	13	14	18	7
	N.Y. Mets (NL)	.257	122	420	63	108	15	7	26	74	47	128	19
1984	N.Y. Mets (NL)	.251	147	522	75	131	27	4	26	97	75	131	27
1985	N.Y. Mets (NL)	.277	111	393	78	109	15	4	29	79	73	96	26
1986	N.Y. Mets (NL)	.259	136	475	76	123	27	5	27	93	72	141	28
1987	N.Y. Mets (NL)	.284	154	532	108	151	32	5	39	104	97	122	36
1988	N.Y. Mets (NL)	.269	153	543	101	146	27	3	39	101	85	127	29
Major League Totals		.266	823	2885	501	768	143	28	186	548	449	745	165

GWRBI: 1983-11; 1984-8; 1985-8; 1986-15; 1987-5; 1988-15. Total: 62

CHAMPIONSHIP SERIES RECORD

YEAR	CLUB	AVG.	G	AB	R	H	2B	3B	HR	RBI	BB	SO	SB
1986	Mets vs. Astros	.227	6	22	4	5	1	0	2	5	3	12	1
1988	Mets vs. Dodgers	.346	7	30	4	9	2	0	1	6	2	4	0

WORLD SERIES RECORD

YEAR	CLUB	AVG.	G	AB	R	H	2B	3B	HR	RBI	BB	SO	SB
1986	Mets vs. Red Sox	.208	7	24	4	5	1	0	1	1	4	6	3

ALL-STAR GAME RECORD

YEAR	CLUB	AVG.	G	AB	R	H	2B	3B	HR	RBI	BB	SO	SB
1984	N.L., Mets	.500	1	2	0	1	0	0	0	0	0	1	0
1985	N.L., Mets	1.000	1	1	2	1	0	0	0	0	1	0	1
1986	N.L., Mets	.500	1	2	1	1	0	0	0	0	0	0	0
1987	N.L., Mets	.000	1	2	0	0	0	0	0	0	0	1	0
1988	N.L., Mets	.250	1	4	0	1	0	0	0	0	0	1	1
Totals		.363	5	11	2	4	0	0	0	0	1	3	1

ROGER CLEMENS—1989 RECORD SHEET

APPEARANCES	W/L	ERA	GS	CG	SHO	SV	IP	HR	ER	BB	SO
1											
2											
3											
4											
5											
6											
7											
8											
9											
10											
11											
12											
13											
14											
15											
16											
17											
18											
19											
20											
21											
22											
23											
24											
25											
26											
27											
28											
TOTALS											

DARRYL STRAWBERRY—1989 RECORD SHEET

WEEK-BY-WEEK	AVG	G	AB	R	H	2B	3B	HR	RBI	BB	SO	SB
1												
2												
3												
4												
5												
6												
7												
8												
9												
10												
11												
12												
13												
14												
15												
16												
17												
18												
19												
20												
21												
22												
23												
24												
25												
26												
27												
28												
TOTALS